# NOTHING BUT LIGHT

*Books by Robert Pack*

# NOTHING BUT LIGHT

". . . your face tells us
something we must forget to live."
—LAWRENCE RAAB

## ROBERT PACK

RUTGERS UNIVERSITY PRESS

*New Brunswick, New Jersey*

The poems in this volume have appeared in the following maga-
zines and anthologies, whose editors the author wishes to thank:
*Antaeus, Antioch Review, Countermeasures, The Denver Quar-
terly, Harper's Magazine, Modern Occasions, The New York
Quarterly, Poetry Magazine, The Poetry Miscellany, Poetry
Northwest, The Random House Book of Contemporary Ameri-
can Poetry, The Saturday Review,* and *The Southern Review.*

*Library of Congress Cataloging in Publication Data*

Pack, Robert, 1929–
  Nothing but light.

  Poems.
  I. Title.
PS3531.A17N6        811'.5'4        72-7403
ISBN 0-8135-0738-3

*For Marion and Elliot Howard*

# CONTENTS

## I

## II

## III

# NOTHING BUT LIGHT

I

# WERE IT NOT

For rumors of war and wars
                          men against men
I think I could grow
                          gracefully back to earth
This morning warm
                          for April in Vermont
Graceful I sit in the sun
                          nuzzling a pear
Warming my teeth my tongue
                          to my body's roots
Wet it is warm and wet
                          it flows it is good
For the grip of my roots
                          here on this morning
In this sun in this sprouting
                          April returning now
Here I am sower of children
                          there they are
My wife has invented
                          coffee again butter bread
They are good and she is good
                          and my children
Have redeemed all sorrow now
                          one bad blood night ago
Now all is grace
                          sun surges in each dew
Nothing can spoil this now
                          you are all
Every one of you
                          all all are invited
This warm morning
                          to my house

# THE PACK RAT

Collector of lost beads, buttons, bird bones,
Catalogue-maker with an eye for glitter,
Litter lover, entrepreneur of waste—
Bits of snail-shell, chips of jugs, red thread,
Blue thread, tinfoil, teeth; fair-minded thief
(Leaving in my pocket when I slept,
A pine cone and two nuts for the dime you stole);
Reasonable romancer, journeying more
Than half a mile to meet a mate, split-eared
Lover with a bitten tail (your mate mates rough),
You last all courtship long, you stick around
When the brood comes, unlike most other rats;
Payer of prices, busy with no dreams,
But brain enough to get along; moderate
Music maker with moderate powers, thumping
The drum of frightened ground with both hind feet
Or scraping dry leaves till the still woods chirp;
Simple screamer seized by the owl's descent,
One scream and one regret, just one; fellow,
Forebear, survivor, have I lost my way?

# TOGETHER WE LAY DOWN

Together we lay down where time begins
Where time has gone a limb sprouts from a pear
Our kisses taught us all the outs and ins
Coming and going always found us there

To hold back is to touch as touchers know
Where time renews a trunk sprouts from a limb
Such growing backwards taught our bodies so
To lose a him in her and her in him

Time gathers to a pause where trunk strikes ground
There is a double speed in going slow
We stopped to find our coming turned around
A pear was what we were where we would go

The seed is in the ground all come to kiss
Where time stops we lie down no end to this

# MY DAUGHTER

The odor of limp leaves
   from the drenched (November) lawn
Reminds me there is time
   to stop (inside) to pause
Watching you (by the window)
   gathering in all I need
To go on.
   Wrapped (for an instant)
In yourself
   you hold your green stuffed bird
As still as he
   believing he can fly
(That you can fly?).
   Only for an instant
I pause limp
   in your second year
As the leaves lie
   in the November morning mist
Their odor thickening
   (perhaps I imagine it)
Pouring in the window
   filling my mouth my breath
As I watch your breathing
   as I go on watching.
I am pouring out of myself
   my wounds open
But I am not hurt—
   what cure is this
What shall I do with my hands
   (shall I put them
In the fountain shall I heal
   the trees)? Twitching
His tail feathers the green bird
   scratches the leaves

The leaves fly up into the trees
  the fountain (where you sit)
Is singing
  angels are there
They pause to drink
  and the water pleases them.
Daughter what have you done
  I cannot go on watching
My hands are limp
  they would fly from me
To you
  as birds fly (as angels fly).
Do you see them in your hair
  do you know who I am
Who must turn away
  as you rise (with your stuffed bird)
As your second year goes on
  and I go on
Though I am healed
  and all others (in November)
Who believe me.

# THE MOUNTAIN ASH TREE

It is silent January
        but on the ash tree
                the orange berries
        are still hanging.
Who decided this
        there is no purpose in it
                though I can imagine
        each to be a globe of blood
a soldier's epitaph or
        a sparrow's or your own.
                What is the point—
        that we live to die
and die to be remembered
        for some purpose
                in a globe of blood?
        I have no purpose
though here I am
        remembering you
                remembering
        the ash tree
while it is there
        outside and down a hill.
                The winter sun is still
        a great light
in the heavens.
        It says to me behold
                the orange berries
        which I recall to do.
It says see
        they are not alive
                though there they are
        to console
or to bring back sorrow
        as you so choose.

                    I try
            I say to myself
as the sun speaks
            (many beasts and men
                        and worlds
            have died in its sight)
that soldier there
            is not your son
                        you are not
            the sparrow's wife.
But sorrow returns
            there is no
                        escaping it—
            the sorrows of other men
almost your own
            the sorrows of small birds
                        and the beasts of the field.
            I shall remake the world.
I shall cleanse the waters.
            The sun says
                        let it be so.
            I shall make pure the air.
That too is good
            says the sun.
                        Cities shall be gardens
            and only natural death
shall live.
            I approve that
                        best of all
            the sun says
and the ash shall flourish
            and the sparrow breed
                        and the soldier
            shall lie down whole
in his own bed.

But that does not
                console—
it cannot be.
I must
        without purpose without hope
                find something
        to hold to
as I hold
        to you
                and you to me
        while we go down.
I open the door on sunlight
        I walk in the field
                through the snow
        down to the ash tree
I put a berry
        in my mouth
                I bite it
        it is hard and bitter
and without purpose
        and I stand there
                your image white in my eyes
        saying to the sun
I am still alive.

# FOR THIS MOMENT

I am walking
in another life
having forsaken you
who have loved me
and helped me
and chosen to live
only in the life
I have this moment
abandoned.

Am I looking
for immortality
that I might return
bearing a gift
a red flower you have never
seen before?

Would you recognize me?

I fear that already
I have been gone
too long.

# EVERYTHING IS POSSIBLE

I am becoming a god!
At last!
I knew I could make it.
You always told me so.
I knew I could never rest
Until I did it.
Now in my left hand, see
My first made meadow.
Let there be a fox
With a magnificent, wandering, rufous tail
Echoing windward behind it.
Does that please you?
And behind that stone
I have shaped
Like a head emerging
From the bristle of cut sheaves
Is the vixen's den lit
With the polished eyes of her cubs.
Do you like that?
And there in repose in my right hand
Pulses a lake,
You can hear the roots
Of the willow trees sucking
Toward the source of its flow.
What color fish
Shall I put in it?
Shall I make them symmetrical?
Shall I fleck them
With random dots
And inscrutable blotches?
Everything is possible!
You always told me so.
Let there be a child!
May I plant him inside you
And let him grow

To tend the fox and tend the fish,
Humming the meadow,
Whistling the shape of the lake?
Could we rest then?
Would you like that?
Would that then make us free?

*For John Conron*

# THE HUMMINGBIRD

hums with her wings, I am
   in flight again. Surely
I can master the air suspended
   at a rose to stay
while the sun pivots around me
   another hour, another day.
I have entered her heart within
   a fraction of an inch,
within her nest no larger
   than a walnut shell, laced
with lichen and with spider webs,
   while wind bulges,
leaves blare and the petaled sun
   pivots around me. My wings,
you cannot see them move, I am here to stay
   as the rose lifts up
forever in the sun. I pivot
   to my nest, warming
two unbelievably tiny eggs,
   for that is the way,
it must be repeated at another hour
   on another day.
Having entered her heart, the heart of the rose,
   I whirl with the sun,
I enter humming two tiny eggs
   repeating the way
as the rose lifts mastering the air,
   suspended in the sun
in flight unbelievably with wings—
   a hummingbird

who hums the ruby color at his throat
   sipping the rose
as I hum sipping at the sun.
   I enter his heart, her heart,
their nest, their eggs, I am in flight
   until the petals
unbelievably burn away
   in the humming air
at another hour on another day.

# INSIDE MY HOUSE

a humid, small wind,
breathing its glitter of dust,
is humming a theme
I have not yet devoured.
Its lips are ripe,
made, as they are,
of nothing,
of what I choose—
made of your lips
which have swallowed each silence
I owned, welcoming me.
I enter the wind's ear
gently, you have shown me how
to be gentle,
though I am grim to see the theme
glittering, to see it
grimly silent before
I choose your eyes
to show me
how my coming looks.
Yes, the wind is breathing its dust
whose taste fills me,
whose lips tell me
*hum softly a little*
*make yourself gentle*
*lie down in all the spaces*
*where the moisture gathers*
*and is gone.*

# WHO WILL LOVE ME?

Who will love me,
whom can I touch,
if you choose to wed yourself
to sorrow
your inexhaustible lover?

Meet me beside those twin
familiar trees,
where the stream turns south,
that seem to be
exchanging branches,
though the stark elm
goes on being dead,
and the October Maple
blossoms its leaves for both.

I shall confess a secret.
I also slept with sorrow,
wooed its unwithering blooms.

I shall rise out of my past
to marry you.
I shall swallow the wind.
I shall suck up the waters.
I shall think nothing but leaves.
The elm must be cut down.
Nothing but leaves and our
breathing, flowering, touching.

# THE MOMENT AFTER

You are gone. Lately I am left
    in a circle of trees:
I am with your absence in a space
    I had to imagine.
The pine needles glare, one by one
    they are emerging
From the mist—or are being engulfed.
    Perhaps it is autumn.
Preceded by his cry, a crow appears,
    vanishes, his cry
Trailing after him, his shadow
    in my eyes
Which see that you are gone except
    for your faint hands
Which the mist has not yet taken away,
    not yet given back.
I have loved you—I love you forever
    for as long as I can.

*And again I say unto you, it is easier for a camel to go through the eye of a needle, than for a rich man to enter into the kingdom of God.*

## A TRICK

How can you trust my fabulous love if
    I know no tricks?
There! I have ridden a camel through the eye
    of a needle!
Do not be afraid. I have performed
    a poor miracle.
It is a trick of gathering oneself
    into what one believes
And stepping forth. A thousand pardons!
    A thousand pardons!
I have made it sound easier than it is,
    and no longer
Do you trust me? I am poor without you, follow me,
    do not turn away.
And so you cannot. And so you need
    my needing you.
We are wedded to each other, first and last,
    and are rich in that—
Another trick if you consent to it:
    that is your miracle,
Though I fear you for it, for slowly as I speak
    I am coming
To believe you. Come, come—I will not
    turn away,
I have no place to go, and I forgot to say
    there is no passing back
Through the needle's eye, now that I am rich
    with you beside me.

Take it! Prick your finger! That is
    my ring of blood,
I see it in the veins of your eyes,
    in the veins of your hands,
In your blue breast veins where the world's
    children nurse
Sucking in no fear. Forgive me! What miracle
    have I conjured up
On the other side of the needle's eye
    too easy too poor
To believe, not to be trusted in the veins
    of your hands
Or the veins of your eyes? I have lied,
    I live by a lie,
And you are free now to return
    through the needle's eye,
As I am free, though you turn to see
    if I am following,
And I follow with a ring of rich blood
    on my finger,
Riding my camel, my own hot beast,
    singing
The first miracle and the last.

# AT THIS DISTANCE

it is difficult to tell
whether you are approaching
    or moving away.
Noon sunlight on the snow,
    the still field nothing
but light, holds you
    where you are,
a dark form that keeps my eyes
    from closing.
Suddenly I know
    you are returning
with great news, something
    that will change
our lives, a flower,
    never found before,
having pierced the snow,
    whose violent odor
restores a past
    in which we start again.
As if from underground
    wind lunges and blurs,
the whole field
    seems to lift up,
tilting away from me.
    You struggle,
holding the flower
    from the wind, pushing
but moving backward.
    *Throw it away!*
*Do not breathe it*
    *without me!*
The wind twists gouging
    into its hole,
the field tilts back,
    nothing but light.

If it is not too late,
    if you return,
I will offer you
    a single bloom,
one with no power, smelling
    only of plucked light.

# BREAKFAST CHERRIES

I am the breakfast poet. I eat everything.
  I have chosen again
to will to hold on, composing my voice.
  This is my last meal,
my children's random quarreling, the same
  last meal that I ate
yesterday. Join me, be with me, gladden
  your tongue with ripe words,
though only the sun, the whitening sun, shimmers
  the cherries all at once
in their yellow porcelain bowl. They shimmer darkly
  and do not go out
as my children's voices, now blue incense, taking
  and exchanging shapes,
mingle above the cherries, pushing, complaining
  to commence the day.
They are happy, though it is only another morning
  that begins, another
last day and again a final meal to share
  as cherry-pits
harmonize whitening songs in the white sun
  in the porcelain bowl, my poem,
singing what I (what we) will them to sing
  with their children's skulls.
Paradise, in its day, sounded like this,
  darkening cherries
were eaten there, and the pits were thrown away
  with their songs. Nothing
was designed to last, not even the sun, why
  should I quarrel with that?
Now orioles flute in the outside spaces
  unseen, so near,
and falling away. The children listen. I listen
  to their listening

as you approach again only to complain
   that I have wandered off,
bearing your gifts, your cherries, so I return
   to eat, faithful again.
Cherry-pits flow from the porcelain bowl, they cover
   the carpet, they are in my bed;
and now only cherry trees flutter the field,
   drifting into the air,
filling the sun as it blooms red and redder.
   I can eat no more.
It is time for school. The children are quarreling,
   cherry-pits in their kisses,
orioles in their ears. Join me, be with me, hold on,
   we have everything to lose.

II

# THE BOX

I open the lock of the box,
where I have kept my goals,
preserving them intact
should I ever need them.
How pretty they are
with their fixed eyes
and their folded hands!
I have not the heart
to disturb them, they are serious
and happy. I blow in the ear
of my favorite, it smiles comfortably.
I run my tongue up another's arm,
its adoring look is unchanged.
Good my dears, I have trained you well
over and over so long ago.
Sleep sleep and be true!
I lock the box, removing
gently a little wind,
and swiftly walk forever
to the next loud room
where my children play,
placing me and me and me
in their eyes in their ears in a box,
weeping and laughing,
preserving my goals.

# SONG TO MYSELF

I take a knife and cut my finger off.
It does not bleed. The cut is in my mind:
The doctor holds my pulse and makes me cough.
He says there is a cure for going blind.

I come to blame for all the hate men grow.
Is that hate harbored if I make it mine?
I grow by choosing what I choose to know.
Blood in my eyes reflects the world's blood shine.

We must stop killing. How can that be done?
Is it too soon to stop, is it too late?
The doctor says my finger is a gun.
Who grew it as an instrument of hate?

No good, no good, to harbor hate alone!
If that is pride, I know the seed of doom.
I must sail down into each cell and bone,
And feel good darkness cleansing in my room.

But not to kill myself, and not to kill,
And not to hate bone death which is the same.
There is good dark blood flowing in my will.
I name it friendship and it grows that name.

I say this to myself that I may live,
That I may harbor children sailing free.
A seed blooms out the music good hands give.
I reach this flowing to you. Answer me.

# APOCALYPSE IN BLACK AND WHITE

When all the rubble of our fears was piled
Smoke upon dust, white silence upon smoke,
And one black horse reined loose by one white child
Broke by as black the bleating white waves broke,
Amid the first, the last, the dying dead,
All burning voices burned into my head.

One silenced cry, one charred black mouth, was all,
Its voices cinders searing my white eyes.
We wailed together at the wailing wall,
Blood from our hands and hearts smoking the skies,
And all the dead with all that dying spent
Cried out this death was more than death had meant.

Into the rubbled wall, the smoke, the waves,
Rode one black child spurred free on his white horse,
The white-charred men burned down in their black graves,
Fear of white death had finished its black course;
One hope, one fate, one death, one brotherhood
Was all I saw, and all I understood.

*For David Littlefield*

## A SIMPLE QUESTION

I open the window on broad noon. Ah,
    busy the sun!
Let the sun thrive and the air drink deep,
    and all breathe, all breathe!
The ships come to my sill, feeding on seeds,
    and the planes come down
Nuzzling my flowers, chanting their grateful hymns.
    And the tractors come,
And the trains poke up from the ground, delighted,
    blinking their eyes, sniffing—
I feed them from my hand, I give them
    what I have
And they praise me. And in the yard the cars
    are snorting laughing
Gamboling like elephants, while buses
    chase and are chased,
Animal and child, stone and tree,
    romping together.
How have I done this? I have loved them all
    and they obey me,
Sharing my burdens and the oldest comfort
    of good works,
Playing and building, resting into song.
    We are one,
We gather at dinner time, we talk by the moon,
    I too have thanks to offer,
Though they prefer I do not speak of it,
    but the bond is there,
Like the sun we breathe and the stars and the sound
    of the night wind,

And when time comes for them to sleep
  I tell them all
They have done well, that I have needed them.
  What is this talk of worlds
Where creature and creator fall apart,
  How can that be
When all things love what loves them,
  need what needs them?
This fear is new to me. I place on the table
  my first ocean,
Open it to see if something deep inside
  may possibly go wrong,
The fish leap out and back, the birds as they should
  come clamoring
Into the air, the rhinoceros rumble
  on the shore
Thundering delight in their own strength,
  the tractors grind
Onto the rocks and up the cliffs, looking,
  asking for work to do.
What can go wrong? Have I asked too much of them?
  Have I given them
Praise enough? Why should they be unwilling
  to work and to die?

33

# LET THERE BE SNOW!

Snow in the hemlocks, more snow still;
Nothing but snow and hemlocks fill my sight.
    "Let more snow in!" I think I will,
        And let my mind blow white.

The night has splintered into snow;
Nothing but hemlocks stop its strict descent.
    My white eyes whiten as they flow
        To find the wind's intent.

"More snow! More snow!" And nothing less
Than every whiteness where wind ever was
    Wakes in my eyes to blind or bless
        The darkness of my cause.

The snow now hurtles from my eyes.
I can do nothing. Nothing now can stop.
    The hemlock trees are hair and thighs,
        And in I drop.

# THE CHILDREN

The children are burning
I must stop it
I must stop it at once
though they are not
my own
not yet my own
yet I do care
I must choose to care
they are all innocent.
We must go backwards
we must return
to a simpler time
was there ever
such a time
and if not
if such time never was
a time without care
can I still believe
that it might have been
and if so
set out to find it?
But the children are burning
their faces like wrinkled fruit
their eyes sizzle
their lips burst
now even as I speak
as I compose myself
to find the facts
and judge and in judging
kill
and in killing
stop the killing
bringing back
that carefree time
that never was
though I believe it

                    if only
            for the children's sakes.
Fool fool
                    I cannot kill
            my way backwards
to fruitful innocence
                    what temptation
            have I eaten
what careless dream
                    have I composed
            that I might kill
in righteousness
                    in innocence
            to save the world
the garden
                    dead almost to its roots
            with all its holy devils
for were they too
                    not children once
            and have they not
children they care for
                    of their own
            who will be burned
burning with my own
                    as we all burn down
            in the carefree flames
with the odor of fruit
                    with nothing to save us
            nothing
but pity and remorse
                    composed at last
            as we stop to look back
at what we cared for.

## PREPARING FOR WINTER

Though the frosted willow is now half yellow,
the silent lawn once more must be mowed.
I must scatter the whispering seeds by hand
in the bare places for the long slant snows
to drive down in. I must think about the next
new season. The garden must be plowed under.
Sunflower seeds for the chickadees.
I want their two songs. Fruit trees must be wrapped
or the rabbits will gnaw them, girdle their barks
and kill their dreams. Once more I must decide
what to protect. I must split and stack dry wood
beneath the shed. When the electric power
goes off, and blown snow blocks my road, I must
have fire. I must think about the next new season.
I want to live here. I want to survive.
What if there were no one else, no seeds?
I must want to survive. The next new lawn.
Two songs of the chickadees. Two songs.

# MY SPIDER

The web I watched my spider spin
  Weaved over her right eye.
It seemed a good way to begin
To help her keep some darkness in
  That she could love me by.

And next my spider spanned her nose
  To seal her nostrils up,
But as the web began to close
A little dew of breath arose;
  I caught it in a cup.

I drank it down, my spider leapt
  Upon her lowered lip
And cast its thread where I had kept
My nursing mouth before it slept
  Withdrawing tip from tip.

Her darkness had become my own,
  I held it in my sleep;
Her dew wrapped up for me alone
Hardened to an egg of bone
  For me to wake—or keep.

# AN EXERCISE

I bring you an exercise
That works. I bring you a spiritual exercise.
  Let go! Let the worms
Crawl out of your eyes, the ants from your ears—
  you are not responsible
For their growing there. Cleanse yourself!
  When you are clean of guilt
You will be ready to live forever.
  Moving your bowels,
Make sure you push the last coins out. Beware
  of parasitic pennies,
They will remain, breeding inside you.
  Your parents are to blame,
And your parents' parents, they have fed you too long
  on possessive love.
Disown the past where the unrepentant dead
  still fornicate.
There is no history in paradise—
  you will be yourself
Over and over. But you must let go, you must
  hold to nothing.
That bear in your chest eating your heart's honey,
  banish him,
Though he will go mad, tearing at the roots
  of the city,
Whimpering beneath his screams. Let him go,
  his freedom is your own,
Though he be homesick for the honey
  of your heart.
That lion in the buzzing shade of your groin,
  that tropical glen,
What will you do with him? Peel your name
  from his nose,
From his belly, from his tail, he is not yours,
  forget him,

39

Cut him from your dreams. Ah, you are learning,
   the exercise
Soon will be habit, soon will the need for thought
   fall easily away.
One final effort, and you are free,
   is still required.
The worms you have cast out, where have you put them?
   In the earth?
No, that will not do! They will flourish there
   eating on ants,
On bears, on lions, eating on worms.
   You must scorch them out,
You must cleanse the earth, all graves must be abolished
   where all men eat to die.
Let death go! I come to tell you this,
   immortal,
Having fasted my entire life.

# MOVIE SCENE

Mellifluous, his voice darkens the room.
The finished turkey stirs in the candle-light.
He squints through the pistol-barrel, explaining
The president's words to her. The nation
Must be preserved. That means war. Her arms
Tuck under her gingham bosom, she rustles
To the window, startles the curtain, peers out
At the glum rain. Johnny has snuck down-stairs,
Standing spread-eagle in his red pajamas.
He buckles his toy holster on, watching
Him kiss her mouth as a gust from the opened door
Flops the letter from her hand across
The room. Flames spit in the stone fireplace.
And he is gone into the storm's low growl,
The whinny, and the clatter away of hoofbeats.
She turns, her lost words stifled in her eyes,
Her perfect face comes closer: the starched cheek
And the still curl stiff over her forehead.
"Get 'em, Daddy, get 'em!" shoots Johnny's gun.

*Father, come back, we must remake the past!*

# AT THE CONCERT

The retarded girl, breasted full
   as a woman,
Sucks at her lolly softly as she is able.
   She has been taught.
Orange saliva slips over her hung chin.
Her mother, with perfected patience, dabs it
   and closes her kept hands
Dead center over her plumped-up lap,
Listening to the free water-frolic
   of melodic flute runs.
It is her love that makes the child behave
   as if listening,
And the child's love that she obeys.
   The oboeist's lips
Have forgotten the labor of learned control,
And now, for this moment, he floats content
   in his minor air.
Like everyone else, the child applauds; I applaud.
   She has behaved well.
And I. She waves, a smile unburdening
Her eyes, to the departing musicians.
   Her mother lowers her hand.
I reach out—I would take them both home.
   But the concert
Is gone. My hands will never be free.

# THE JUDGE

Softly I approach the safe
where my reason,
with its sentences, its laws,
is filed:
three to the left, once around,
three to the right,
and softly *click*.
When I used it last,
you convicted me,
hunching your brows,
shaking your red beard,
and I was hanged,
my penis erect,
my tongue limp.
Such deaths do not last long
if one thinks them out.
And now, this time again,
I have been tried, concluding
reason's proper use
is softly to defy defy defy.
I shave clean my head,
I stitch up my ears—
there is no place for you to enter
with your poisonous fluid,
your condition.
Notch by notch, I have chosen
white silence:
three to the left, once around,
three to the right,
then silence, deeper and more.
Whatever your red words say,
I will never again
be merciful.

# TO AN UNKNOWN READER

In this thin haze, in this moist cloudy light,
The Green Mountain range again seems blue.
I have not figured out why this glazed sight
Makes me speak to myself or speak to you.
Tight buds on the birches show faint signs of swelling.
It is hushed March. A few stray flakes are falling.

You can see them without my saying so—
And yes, of course, in March the birch buds swell
And in this haze eke out a pale rose glow
To say the season turneth, all is well.
The Green Mountains seem to shift their hue;
Now in my eyes they are more mauve than blue.

The Green Mountains! From here they are not green.
What am I trying to see or trying to say—
That I do not know your name or what you mean?
Will you murder me if I stop in your way?
The season turneth, but is that what I see?
Now in this haze there burns a red birch tree.

It burns in oranges without a voice.
The mountains are no longer far away.
Within the flames I think I see your face—
Or is it mine? What has it come to say?
The Green Mountains come—the flames' black cover:
A human season turneth, and is over.

# THE RULER

Having wandered through the tumult city,
  having asked why men,
Afraid of death, are not afraid to kill,
  having pondered it
And cast my vote, I arrive again
  renewing myself
At the bed where I buried my first lost tooth.
  Behold! I remove the pillow,
It is still there, obdurate and gleaming,
  reflecting old wishes,
Old defeats. I must confront them. I must
  discipline myself.
I must return to the source of things,
  to the source of eating
And the course and end of appetite
  if I am to rule.
And so I do—I replace my new tooth
  with the old,
Fitting it carefully, molding the gum
  around it, tapping,
Stanching the blood. The tooth begins to throb
  with memory:
My mother with an ice-pack on my cheek,
  my father glowering
Disapproval at my screams. Behold!
  I have caught them
Each in an eternal pose, I have set
  all of us free!
We know now what we are and can
  transform ourselves.
Discipline! I have done it with discipline!
  I shall rule you all,
Having mastered myself, having traced the past
  to its hurt roots

And controlled my screams. I shall finish
   my book explaining
Everything. I shall be elected. The votes
   are streaming in,
The people clamoring for me. They need me.
   I bring them freedom
In a tooth. Behold! In my cupped hands
   there are two teeth,
And four, and now a skull, and now
   a skeleton
Kicking his feet, throwing out his arms,
   screaming *Control yourselves!*

III

# THE SCREECH OWL

With an embryo's face, a wail, the screech owl,
   shredding the night,
opens the tale I live in, having chosen
   to forget, trying
to remember now the humped stone I escaped from
   many shapes ago.
And the mouse returns to his young from the oracle
   where vexed wind taught him
only his own speech and the hunger grip
   with which he arrived
as dust answered with a mouth of dust, with entrails
   where the oak roots groan.
Soon enough we will all meet, the owl inspired
   from his hollow tree,
eyes facing forward, and the mouse blinking,
   repeating to his pulse
the fanged warnings that he learned at birth.
   It is my tale—
it is all inside me—here where a ripped kiss
   begins the world
in my belly where the sea blurts forth and the oak
   roots grapple a stone,
its lips straining toward its thought of the sun.
   Here the prophetic eyes
of the mouse drain backward into my hooked hands
   as the owl retreats alive
with his kill to his young in the hollow tree
   where a stone throbs
at its roots, trying to escape what it must know,
   what I cannot choose
not to remember though all kisses bleed,
   that its tale
will lead it where I am—in the mouse's eyes,
   in the stretched belly

of the owl, to begin again, to choose
   again to continue,
until the screeching sun sucks back the sea.

# I AM RISING

I am rising out
of myself,
leaving my past below—
a sleeping body.

Beneath the eyelids
there is terrible leaping movement—
the same dream of someone
walking slowly slowly slowly
from the room.

Why does he not cry out
or call me back?
Perhaps he imagines
it is he
who is walking naked slowly
from the room?

Shall I kiss him
on the lips
*farewell?*
Shall I fondle his body
to change his dream
as if I were his mother—
or his wife?

If that woke him,
would he know who I was,
would he follow me
out of the room,
or draw me slowly back
to his bare lips,
soothing me to sleep,
whispering *you can stay?*

# HE DIES ALIVE

thinking of brightness, my friend, suckling
  the lemon light,
taking its taste to his roots where the sea drops
  deeper than it remembers.
Now and forever, he dies alive of natural
  man-made causes,
my friend, each one of you, and my cause
  is to speak of it
without weapons in my voice—there is enough
  of that—without blame,
what can blame cure? only to tell
  of the brightness his eyes
and his tongue have forever loved: the lemon light
  and the orange
and the perfect inward glow of the plum
  whose juices flow
deeper than the sea remembers and beyond
  what the stars
shall have time ever to learn to forsake.
  And I praise the brightness
though forever it be lost as the live tongue
  of my friend
withdraws and withers in the star of his head,
  though my cause
cannot rescue his eyes which now are crabs
  and now are stones
and forever now are the sea's lost dream
  of its cause.
And my friend, each one of you, suckles
  his first last look
at the lemon light, touching, being touched,
  as stars ebb
to their roots deeper than the stones remember
  or the sea will have time

to forget. And my cause is to speak
   without blame
of natural man-made causes, weapons, fire,
   hoping only to cure
*forsaking the life* of his tasted last look
   of the lemon light
in the sea of my friend's eyes where the brightness
   now forever burns
in its cause, with each one of you, myself, touching,
   living our only death.

*For Jon and Pamela Powell*

# HER BLACK HAIR

flares gliding in his eyes. The lift of snow,
within the snow's descent, begins again,
again it stops. Four crows. He does not know
he laughs awake. She starts to see him when
snow lunges at the window where he lies.
He strains to touch and wake her with his eyes.

One snowflake fills the mirror and explodes.
The sun flares black. He tumbles toward the sun.
He meets her at the meeting of four roads.
Four crows descend within the snow begun
again he sees her start, she sees him stop.
The mirror meets them rising as they drop.

Four crows are mourning on a hemlock limb.
He starts to stop her weeping as they weep.
He touches her. Four roads. She touches him.
She meets him in the laughter of his sleep.
The window in the mirror starts to flow,
and lifts their falling with the lift of snow.

Again his laughter startles her awake.
The sun spins down. The snow begins to rise.
Behind the lunging mirror four crows break
the light again exploding from his eyes.
There is no stop to starting—they are where
all eyes are suns again. Four roads. Black hair.

# EMPTINESS

is flowing again,
neither closer
nor further away,
neither up nor down;
its red eye is still.
Call it a white bird
whose feathers shift
and remain in place.
The water, or perhaps
the sky, mirrors
the bird's blue poise,
its will to remain.
Another bird,
exactly the same,
joins it and takes its place,
neither lover nor wife,
neither daughter nor son.
Its eye is green—
that does not matter,
nothing has changed.
The poise of the water bird
ceases and continues
if you put it there.

# THE HOLE

Did I choose this? Can my eyes change
    this tightening dark
with a squint? I remember the mole plummeting
    his way to somewhere
his blindness has an image of. Was that me—
    what I have become,
what I choose to follow my way to home
    with darkness turning
on its wheel that has always turned
    as something in me
thrusts upward spinning in the hole
    my brain squints
to discover? And wind turns on its wheel
    rocketing the eyes
of the mole up into his latest dark,
    his deafest space,
circling as he chooses, from the home
    he remembers
and has an image of. And he goes on
    as wind goes on,
his eyes hotter than stars and his starred feet
    still burrowing
to somewhere he has chosen for his change,
    for my change,
though turning darkness plummets me
    into the hole I choose
never to forget. But the mute mole,
    in whose blind voice
I choose to speak of home, in the heat of his need,
    is rocketing
to somewhere I have a falling image of,
    circling on his wheel,
seeking his change, burrowing onward
    deeper into the dark.

# TERMINAL

The voices come to depart, they wait
    rising or falling,
Staring inside. Within the terminal
    they gather rigid
As wooden benches in crowds under clocks
    whose memory has gone out,
Making the private sounds of vanishing
    as they rise or fall
Staying in place. They are all here,
    they have all come
To leave, each one has come, though I cannot
    find you alone among them—
They are all disguised in something about you.
    What can I say,
For whom could I deny your eyes
    that have never chosen
To leave me? My voice rises calling for you—
    how can I save
Everyone? Why have you let this voice
    wear your shoes,
That one your shawl? Or have you come in the glance
    of a child
Still hoping I will seek you here
    and find you?
The voices cry out in a single cry!
    Wearing my father's beard,
The wind arrives with the sea at his lips,
    telling me to forget,
But I cannot forget, and I call for you
    in the only voice I know,
The one that repeats and goes on and repeats
    as the voices turn away
Rising or falling in single file,
    taking you with them.

# BODY PAIN

Whose hurt is this?
What dust-breathed spirit creeps over stones
To inhabit my body, seeking
Its refuge? Are you a god
Who out of personal love
Arrives at last to teach me
What I need to know
In the single language I believe?
Never will I forget again,
Never will my quick bones close their eyes;
Give me more time, give me
My three score years and ten,
And I will use them in the sun's command,
Stroking each moment's fur:
I will go out among the living people,
Seeking each one
Who most resembles you, who most is you,
Having fed you his own breath,
Becoming who you are.
I will inhabit your spirit, learning
Your body's speech
To teach me what I choose to know
Of the refuge in the mortal sun
My bones in their silence
Fail to praise.

# THE RED KNIGHT

A red thought,
            knowing what it knows,
adjusting its eyes,
            arrives
among thickening leaves,
                        expecting me.
I have again determined
                to get there,
not to hold back,
            not to make it wait.
Perhaps I shall kill it,
                or tame it,
for all its red strength,
                though this has never
worked before.
            The survivors,
out of curiosity,
            or boredom,
are attending the event
                I have determined,
I have chosen,
            not to avoid.
They are telling stories
                of what will happen
that they do not
            remember,
having eaten their books.
                And the leaves,
perhaps they are also gone—
                for who can tell,
even by your stomach,
            what is to come?
I do not hold back,
            I will commit myself again,

though these woods
                    will never be safe,
and my eyes
                    are not yet accustomed
to the light
                    shed by these stones,
these survivors
                    who always have been there,
whose minds I am
                    learning to read,
as something in me
                    again moves on,
as I move on, gaining
                    in cunning,
gaining
          in red control.

# THE SPACE

I stare at today's space, shaped
  like an eye.
It is the same space I have memorized
  over and over.
A friend appears—I have never seen before.
  *I come to remind you*
*You must keep your word,* he says, vanishing
  as I recall his hand,
Leaving his space behind, the same space
  I have entered
Over and over. And I enter the surface
  of that space
To save him, trying to imitate his stare
  so he might recall me
If I fail trying to remember him.
  In his hand
A dove appears that never has been born,
  soon to be extinct
Forever—feathers lucent as rain,
  fluttering up
To the edge of his eye and reaching
  like a word
With the same stare in the same place
  which over and over
I enter appearing to recall him
  as a star explodes,
Holding out my hand with a bird soon
  never to be born,
Trying to begin to keep my word,
  trying to begin.

# LEAVING MY FATHER

I must have left him asleep
underneath
the oak's damp voice
where gnarled eyes sat
knowing
what I would do next,
what I had to do.
And I did, though
each time I went on,
the same got more,
and now it has drifted
longer ago
than the oak's vowed voice
can drown
or its eyes can cause me
to cease to repeat.
Dreaming, he is still there
with his puffed lips
repeating *go on, go on,*
*I shall wait*
*as long as you never return;*
with his stopped eyes
remembering
the eyes of the oak
and the oak's foam voice,
knowing
I would continue to come back,
that I had to come back
to bury him
beneath our shaken tree,
so that my eyes, my children,
drifting beyond me,
may learn to forget.

# THE PLEA OF THE WOUND

If only I could remember if
   I got this way
In self defense. And you, if still alive,
   do you mistrust me yet?
Have you forgotten me, speaking as I do?
   Smelling my fate,
The question it asks, the insects sing on.
   Their time has not passed.
My bleeding starts again, it has never stopped,
   has yours stopped?
It is happening. Yes, it is all happening.
   I have said it before
But have never believed it. I shall say it now
   but will not believe it.
And the stunned dinosaurs burrow deeper
   into their tombs,
They have stopped bleeding forever except
   in my blood or yours
If you are still alive, defending
   your right to go on,
Remembering me if I am the one
   who created your hurt voice
Where the insects feed. And your voice sings
   of the pity of it,
Asking forgiveness, asking what have you done
   to me, speaking
In my voice that has tried and is trying
   to remember
The cause that will make it all happen,
   and is happening,
And indeed has already happened even now
   as the insects sing
And the dinosaur oblivion deepens
   into the spaces

Where my bleeding goes unable to remember
   how I got this way,
How I started off with you in this way,
   how this way,
Though I plead against it, leads me on.

# PRAYER TO MY FATHER WHILE PUTTING
## MY SON TO BED

Father of my voice, old humbled ghost,
    ragged with earned earth,
Teach me again to praise those joys
    your last sleep
Still awakes in me. Who am I, mourner,
    to assuage, to contend
With this ravenous year—all the betrayers
    eating the sun?
What can I hold to? What can I tell this boy
    who at moonrise
Picked a vase of asters, purple and white,
    now holding back from sleep
Another trusting moment, listening
    to my voice,
To what it says? Shall my voice, our voice, say
    beware of the betrayer
(In the room of your heart, in this room
    where you brought your asters
Purple and blue and white, those plucked stars),
    I am the one
You have dreamed about who has stolen your waters,
    devoured your air?
That is only the guilty truth, I must
    not go back
To that, mourning your death and his death to come
    I have given birth to,
And the sun's murder which you and I
    and he too
Must commit. But in your memory, father,
    ghost of my voice,
I choose another theme equally old—
    I speak it simply
As I know how, feeling what I feel
    praising the sun

With you awake in my mind and this boy
   here, here
Hugging goodnight, holding the dark,
   his dark and mine,
With his asters lighting this mourning room
   for you old humbled ghost—
It is good, what I feel is good, I feel
   it has always been good.
I hold to it as you held to it. If only
   my voice, this poem,
This prayer, could hold you back in life,
   and protect my child
When another and another morning comes.

# NOW FULL OF SILENCES

Now full of silences, now full of sighs,
    as light wind lifts
Over stones shining like little moons,
    the lumbering animals come,
Filling the last spaces, to enact our fate.
    They come in pairs
As they have always done, freely
    without choice,
Without delay, without the words
    for necessary doom
Which tell our tale, and their tale,
    and the story
Of the gods who once watered here
    sharing their sighs
At the taking off of immortality.
    Never abandoning
The past, here we are as the stars shudder
    in a different element
Keeping watch over the stony fields
    we are learning to forego
As the animals leave for the last spaces
    full of silences
Which our words fill emptying themselves,
    watering the final pity
We once taught the gods when we walked
    among them.
I cry out for the animals to hear—
    that I am with them,
That never in my heart have I left them
    or abandoned our tale
And its past that rivals the fertile stars.
    But the animals,
Their blazing bodies dazzling the wind
    I will always remember,

Do not understand, and I cannot explain
    as I tell this tale
With the animal history of love in my eyes.
    I lead them now
Into the story which I cannot choose
    to abandon,
Seeking the sighs gods use to speak
    farewell
That will bind us forever in the silent spaces
    of holy remorse
Where the wind settles and the stones stare
    from their pallid light,
And hand in hand, as we have always done,
    we walk into the past.

## ABOUT THE AUTHOR

Robert Pack is a member of the English faculty at Middlebury
College and Director of the Bread Loaf Writers' Conference. He
holds degrees from Dartmouth College and Columbia University
and has taught at Barnard College.

*The text of this book was set in Baskerville Linotype and printed by Offset on Warren's #66 Antique manufactured by S. D. Warren Company, Boston, Mass. Composed, printed and bound by Quinn & Boden Company, Inc., Rahway, N.J.*

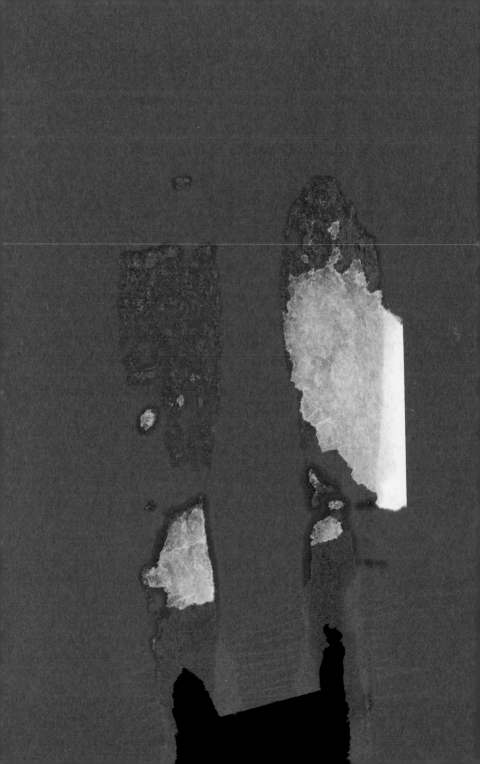